Table of Contents

3

INTRODUCTION

The Dr. Now Diet is a very restrictive low carb, low calorie diet.

Dr. Nowzaradan is a Houston-based bariatric surgeon who specializes in weight loss surgery for people with morbid obesity.

Dr. Now's diet plan aims to help one lose weight by reducing calorie intake.

Although this diet plan can be followed by anyone, it is best suited for overweight or obese people who want to lose weight.

The primary concept of Dr. Now's diet plan is to reduce calorie intake to about 1200 calories a day, without excluding any food groups, except sugar.

The diet encourages patients to reduce calorie intake and eat a healthy balanced diet. This helps them lose weight, the healthy way.

Dr. Now is well known because he takes on patients many other surgeons think are too risky to operate on.

Before the patients have surgery, many of them need to lose weight to reduce their risk of complications and show they'll be able to make the lifestyle changes doctors prescribe after surgery.

Dr. Now puts the patients on a strict low carb and low calorie diet to help them quickly lose weight in preparation for surgery.

HOW TO FOLLOW IT

this book explains the three main principles of his diet approach using the acronym "FAT":

• Frequency. This refers to how often you eat. Dr. Now recommends eating two to three meals per day with no snacks.

• Amount. This means how many calories you should consume. He says to limit calorie intake to 1,200 calories or less each day, divided evenly — so 400 calories for each meal 3 times daily, or 600 calories for each meal twice daily.

• Type. The types of food you eat are also important. He says to strictly avoid sugar and choose low fat and low carb foods while increasing the protein and fiber content of each of your meals. Protein and fiber can help make your meal more filling.

Dr. Now says that when you begin, make a list of all of your favorite foods, and then remove all the sugary, high fat, and high calorie foods from the list.

What remains should be a regular part of your daily meals while you're doing the Dr. Now program — that way, it's easier to stick to.

He also says to focus on minimally processed food and choose small portions, which will help make it easier to meet the restricted calorie count.

This diet is designed for short-term use in the lead-up to bariatric surgery, so don't follow it for longer than a month or two.

Always make sure you're under close medical supervision while you're on this diet.

BENEFITS

This strict, low calorie diet plan does result in fast weight loss, especially in people with higher body weight.

Dr. Now encourages many of his patients who weigh more than 600 pounds (272 kg) to try to lose 30 pounds (14 kg) in just 30 days, and many of them are successful.

In fact, the 1,200 calorie diet is commonly used for preoperative bariatric surgery patients, not just in Dr. Now's practice.

In one study on 24 women with obesity, participants lost a significant amount of weight with and without exercise in just 13 days.

Doctors often recommend preoperative weight loss for people undergoing bariatric surgery because it appears to help reduce complications after the operation.

One study looked at outcomes in more than 480,000 people who had bariatric surgery. The researchers found that weight loss prior to surgery helped reduce the risk of death within 30 days of surgery — even when people lost less than 5% of their body weight.

Studies have also found that when people were re□uired to lose weight before they were approved to have weight loss surgery, they tended to have more successful weight outcomes after surgery.

DOWNSIDES
The Dr. Now Diet plan isn't a good choice, except for those who need to lose weight to have a safe operation.

The 1,200 calorie limit is excessively restrictive for most people and therefore not sustainable.

In fact, long-term extreme calorie restriction might make it harder for you to lose weight.

That's because your body adapts to calorie restriction by slowing down your metabolic rate, meaning you burn fewer calories. Low calorie diets may also affect your hunger hormones, making you hungrier than normal.

Research shows that many of these diets lead to rebound weight gain because of these metabolic changes. As a result, this and other crash diets aren't a good choice if your goal is long-lasting weight loss.

Additionally, very calorie-restricted diets often provide inade□uate amounts of nutrients, even if they're rich in nutrient-dense fruits and vegetables.

For example, one study noted that a high protein, low carb, 1,200 calorie diet — similar to the one Dr. Now recommends — came up short on thiamine, vitamin D, vitamin E, calcium, magnesium, and potassium.

While these gaps may not pose immediate health risks, they could lead to complications in individuals following the diet for more than a short-term basis of a few weeks.

Restrictive diets also cause changes to the gut microbiota, the beneficial bacteria that populate your large intestine.

Maintaining a healthy balance of these gut bacteria is crucial for optimal health and digestion. However, restrictive diets may reduce both the overall population and the diversity of the bacteria present.

Finally, don't attempt the Dr. Now Diet without medical supervision, especially if you have any medical conditions or are taking medications. If you're looking to try this diet, be sure to speak with a healthcare professional beforehand.

FOODS TO EAT

Dr. Now's diet plan allows these foods, along with other high fiber, high protein, low fat, and sugar-free foods.

• **Lean protein sources:** egg whites, lean cuts of meat, chicken breast, turkey breast, beans, tofu, fish

• **Fats and oils:** cooking spray, small amounts of oil for cooking

- **Lower sugar fruits**: all whole fruits, except watermelon, cantaloupe, banana, and mango

- **Most vegetables:** all vegetables, except potatoes

- **Certain nuts and seeds:** flax seeds, chia seeds

- **Nonfat dairy:** plain nonfat yogurt, skim milk

- **Whole-grain carbs:** wheat bread, wheat or corn tortillas, whole-wheat pasta in moderation

- Zero-calorie sweeteners

FOODS TO AVOID

Dr. Now provides his patients undergoing bariatric surgery with a list of foods to avoid on the diet. The list includes foods you would expect, like cookies and French fries, but also some surprising foods, like oatmeal, popcorn, and peanuts.

His reasoning is that oatmeal is high in carbs, popcorn is often doused in fat, and peanuts are high in calories and easy to overeat.

Here are the foods to avoid on Dr. Now's diet plan:

- **Some sources of protein:** high carb or sugary protein shakes, high fat meats, processed meats (like hot dogs, bacon, sausage), battered and fried meats (like fried chicken), eggs

- **Some fats and oils:** butter, olive oil, vegetable oils

- **Fruits higher in sugar:** fruit juices, fruit canned in syrup, fruits that have more natural sugar (watermelon, cantaloupe, banana, and mango)

- **Potatoes:** includes French fries

- **Most nuts and seeds:** peanut butter, peanuts, almonds, cashews, pistachios, sunflower seeds

- **Full fat and sweetened dairy:** sweetened yogurt, sorbet, ice cream, milkshakes, chocolate milk, full fat cheese

- **Certain carbs, especially refined products:** crackers, chips, popcorn, white rice, brown rice, waffles and pancakes, white bread, pasta

- **Sugar-containing sweets:** cookies, candy, cakes and pastries, ice cream, honey, syrup

Dr. Now encourages avoiding several nutritious foods due to their calorie content, including eggs, olive oil, nuts, and seeds.

In addition, Dr. Now suggests limiting whole-wheat bread and other whole-grain carbs, although they're not totally banned from the diet.

SAMPLE MEAL PLAN

Here's a sample menu you could follow for 3 days on the Dr. Now Diet. Since there are no snacks allowed on the diet, you'll only see breakfast, lunch, and dinner suggestions below.

DAY 1

• **Breakfast:** 2 ounces (57 grams) egg whites with spinach, mushrooms, and 1 ounce (28 grams) part-skim mozzarella on 2 pieces whole-wheat toast, ready-to-drink low carb protein shake

- **Lunch:** 3 ounces (85 grams) grilled chicken, salad with 2 tbsp. (30 grams) vinaigrette dressing

- **Dinner:** 3 ounces (85 grams) broiled salmon with asparagus

DAY 2

- **Breakfast:** 1 cup (245 grams) plain nonfat yogurt with stevia and 1/2 cup (75 grams) blueberries, 1 cup (240 mL) skim milk, 2 pieces turkey bacon

- **Lunch:** 1 cup (238 grams) tuna salad made with nonfat Greek yogurt instead of mayo, whole-grain pita, celery, and carrots

- **Dinner**: spiralized zucchini with 4 ground turkey meatballs, marinara sauce, and 1 ounce (28 grams) part-skim mozzarella

DAY 3

- **Breakfast:** fruit smoothie with 1 cup (240 mL) skim milk, 1 scoop protein powder, 1 cup (150 grams) strawberries, 1/2 avocado

- **Lunch:** 1 cup (240 grams) broccoli stir-fry with 3 ounces (85 grams) tofu

- **Dinner:** 2 cups (478 grams) low fat chicken and vegetable soup, side salad with 1 tbsp. (15 grams) vinaigrette dressing

DAY 4

- **Breakfast:** 1 cup of skim milk; two pieces of turkey bacon; 1 cup of plain non-fat yogurt; ½ cup of blueberries or blackberries.

- **Lunch:** 1 cup of tuna salad made with non-fat Greek yogurt instead of mayonnaise; whole-grain pita bread, celery and carrots.

- **Dinner:** A side salad with 1 tablespoon of vinaigrette dressing and 2 cups of low-fat chicken and vegetable soup.

DAY 5

- **Breakfast**

1 egg white plus 1 egg (do not fry) — 105 calories

2oz turkey sausage (microwaved or cooked in water) — 130 calories

0.5 low- fat cottage cheese — 90 calories

1 slice whole-wheat toast — 90 calories

Unlimited Black coffee, unsweetened tea, water

• **Lunch**

2 cups spinach,1 cans tuna in water

2 carrots, 1tbsp light mayo, Unlimited unsweetened tea, water

• **Dinner**

2 cups steamed broccoli, 3oz grilled chicken, 1 oz low- fat cheddar cheese, Unlimited unsweetened tea, water

• **Snacks**

1 slice of low-fat Swiss cheese, 2o turkey breast slices

THINGS YOU NEED TO KNOW

• An important factor to remember when following this diet is not to go below 1200 calories a day.

• Going below the 12000 calorie level will not help your body receive nutrients to stay healthy. You must eat a balanced diet that includes all food groups.

• Following the diet can make you feel hungry. However, care should be taken not to go below 1200 calories as it can endanger your health.

• Dr. Now's diet encourages you to adopt new habits and approach to food. This can be useful in helping you control portion size and calorie intake in the future.

- Once you lose weight, you must continue eating a well-balanced diet to stay healthy and maintain an ideal weight.

- It is important to note that this diet can make you feel hungry especially during the initial stages.

- To curb hunger when following this diet, it is advisable that you eat snacks in between meals and increase your water intake.

- Also, ensure that you reduce the intake of calories in a way that best suited to you.

- For instance, if you one of those people who like to have a heavy breakfast, ensure that your lunch and dinner is light.

- However, if you a person, who can skip breakfast, but feel hungry in the evenings, it is recommended that you have a light snack and save calories for dinner.

DR. NOWZARADAN BREAKFAST RECIPE

BLUEBERRY-BANANA OVERNIGHT OATS

INGREDIENTS

- ½ cup unsweetened coconut milk beverage

- ½ cup old-fashioned oats (see Tip)

- ½ tablespoon chia seeds (Optional)

- ½ banana, mashed

- 1 teaspoon maple syrup

- Pinch of salt

- ½ cup fresh blueberries

- 1 tablespoon unsweetened flaked coconut (Optional)

DIRECTIONS

- Step 1

Combine coconut milk, oats, chia seeds (if using), banana, maple syrup and salt in a pint-sized jar and stir. Top with blueberries and coconut, if desired. Cover and refrigerate overnight.

PEANUT BUTTER-BANANA CINNAMON TOAST
INGREDIENTS

- 1 slice whole-wheat bread, toasted

- 1 tablespoon peanut butter

- 1 small banana, sliced

- Cinnamon to taste

DIRECTIONS

- Step 1

Spread toast with peanut butter and top with banana slices. Sprinkle with cinnamon to taste.

MUFFIN-TIN QUICHES WITH SMOKED CHEDDAR & POTATO

INGREDIENTS

- 2 tablespoons extra-virgin olive oil

- 1 ½ cups finely diced red-skinned potatoes

- 1 cup diced red onion

- ¾ teaspoon salt, divided

- 8 large eggs

- 1 cup shredded smoked Cheddar cheese

- ½ cup low-fat milk

- ½ teaspoon ground black pepper

- 1 ½ cups chopped fresh spinach

DIRECTIONS

- Step 1

Preheat oven to 325 degrees F. Coat a 12-cup muffin tin with cooking spray.

- Step 2

Heat oil in a large skillet over medium heat. Add potatoes, onion and 1/4 teaspoon salt and cook, stirring, until the potatoes are just cooked through, about 5 minutes. Remove from heat and let cool 5 minutes.

- Step 3

Whisk eggs, cheese, milk, pepper and the remaining 1/2 teaspoon salt in a large bowl. Stir in spinach and the potato mixture. Divide the quiche mixture among the prepared muffin cups.

- Step 4

Bake until firm to the touch, about 25 minutes. Let stand 5 minutes before removing from the tin.

AVOCADO-EGG TOAST
INGREDIENTS

- ¼ avocado

- ¼ teaspoon ground pepper

- ⅛ teaspoon garlic powder

- 1 slice whole-wheat bread, toasted

- 1 large egg, fried

- 1 teaspoon Sriracha (Optional)

- 1 tablespoon scallion, sliced (Optional)

DIRECTIONS

- Step 1

Combine avocado, pepper and garlic powder in a small bowl and gently mash.

- Step 2

Top toast with the avocado mixture and fried egg. Garnish with Sriracha and scallion, if desired.

BLUEBERRY-PECAN PANCAKES
INGREDIENTS

- 1 cup all-purpose flour

- ½ cup whole-wheat flour

- ½ cup dried blueberries

- 1/2 cup finely chopped pecans, toasted

- 3 tablespoons light brown sugar

- 2 teaspoons baking powder

- 1 teaspoon ground cinnamon

- ½ teaspoon salt

- 2 large eggs

- 2 large egg whites

- 1 ½ cups nonfat buttermilk

- 2 tablespoons canola oil

DIRECTIONS

- Step 1

Whisk all-purpose flour, whole-wheat flour, blueberries, pecans, brown sugar, baking powder, cinnamon and salt in a large bowl.

- Step 2

Whisk eggs, egg whites, buttermilk and oil in a medium bowl. Make a well in the center of the dry ingredients; add wet ingredients and stir until just combined. Use about 1/4 cup batter for each pancake.

SPICY SLAW BOWLS WITH SHRIMP & EDAMAME
INGREDIENTS

- 1 recipe Spicy Cabbage Slaw

- 2 cups frozen shelled edamame, thawed

- 1 medium avocado, diced

- ½ medium lime, juiced

- 12 ounces peeled cooked shrimp

DIRECTIONS

- Step 1

Prepare Spicy Cabbage Slaw. Add edamame; toss and set aside.

- Step 2

Toss avocado with lime juice in a small bowl.

- Step 3

Divide the slaw mixture among 4 containers. Top each with 1/4 of the shrimp (about 3 ounces) and 1/4 of the avocado. Cover and refrigerate until ready to eat.

AIR FRYER FISH
INGREDIENTS

1 (450g) cod, cut into 4 strips

Salt

Freshly ground black pepper

65 g plain flour

1 large egg, beaten

200 g panko bread crumbs

1 tsp. Old Bay seasoning

Lemon wedges, for serving

Tartar sauce, for serving

DIRECTIONS

1. Pat fish dry and season on both sides with salt and pepper.

2. Place flour, egg, and panko in three shallow bowls. Add Old Bay to panko and toss to combine. Working one at a time, coat fish in flour, then in egg, and finally in panko, pressing to coat.

3. Working in batches, place fish in basket of air fryer and cook at 200°C for 10 to 12 minutes, gently flipping halfway through, or until fish is golden and flakes easily with a fork.

4. Serve with lemon wedges and tartar sauce.

GARLIC BEANS
INGREDIENTS

2 tbsp. extra-virgin olive oil

1 large onion, chopped

2 carrots, chopped

2 stalks celery, minced

1/2 tsp. chilli powder

Salt Freshly ground black pepper

1 x 400g can cannellini beans, drained and rinsed

2 cloves garlic, crushed

1 tsp. thyme leaves

1 l low-salt chicken (or vegetable) stock

500 ml water

1/2 large head cabbage, chopped

1 x 400g can chopped tomatoes

Pinch chilli flakes

2 tbsp. freshly chopped parsley, plus more for garnish

DIRECTIONS

1. In a large pot (or casserole dish) over medium heat, heat olive oil. Add onion, carrots, and celery, and season with salt, pepper, and chilli powder. Cook, stirring often, until vegetables are soft, 5 to 6 minutes. Stir in beans, garlic, and thyme and cook until garlic is fragrant, about 30 seconds. Add stock and water, and bring to a simmer.

2. Stir in tomatoes and cabbage and simmer until cabbage is wilted, about 6 minutes.

3. Remove from heat and stir in chilli flakes, and parsley. Season to taste with salt and pepper. Garnish with more parsley, if using.

BEST-EVER FARRO SALAD
INGREDIENTS

200 g whole-grain farro

480 ml low-sodium vegetable stock

1 1/2 tsp. salt

1 Bay leaf

1 large shallot, very thinly sliced

80 ml extra virgin olive oil

3 tbsp. apple cider vinegar

1 tbsp. dijon mustard

2 tsp. honey

Freshly ground black pepper

50 g rocket

1 green apple, chopped

50 g shaved parmesan cheese

5 g freshly chopped basil

5 g freshly chopped parsley

30 g toasted pecans, roughly chopped

DIRECTIONS

1. In a medium saucepan, combine farro, vegetable stock, salt, and bay leaf. Bring to a boil, then reduce to a simmer and let cook, stirring occasionally, until farro is tender and no broth remains, about 30 minutes. When farro is cooked, transfer to a large bowl to cool.

2. In the meantime, make fried shallots: in a small saucepan over medium heat, combine oil and shallots. When the shallots begin to bubble, reduce heat to medium-low and cook, stirring occasionally, until shallots are golden and crisp and golden, 15 to 20 minutes. Remove shallots from oil with a slotted spoon and place on a paper-towel lined plate and season with salt. Let oil cool.

3. Make dressing: in a medium bowl, combine the cooled olive oil with vinegar, mustard, and honey and season with salt and pepper.

4. Assemble salad: combine cooked farro, crispy shallots, rocket, apple, parmesan, basil, parsley, and pecans. Drizzle dressing over salad and toss to coat.

COURGETTE TOMATO BAKE

INGREDIENTS

450 g courgette (about 3 medium), chopped

700 g cherry tomatoes, preferably multi-coloured, halved

2 cloves garlic, crushed

Extra-virgin olive oil, for drizzling

Salt

Freshly ground black pepper

35 g freshly grated Parmesan

2 tbsp. torn basil, for garnish

DIRECTIONS

1. Preheat oven to 180°C (160ºC fan).

2. In a large bowl, combine courgette, tomatoes, garlic and a drizzle of olive oil. Season with salt and pepper and toss to coat.

3. Transfer vegetables to a small baking dish, then sprinkle with Parmesan. Bake until golden, 33 to 35 minutes.

4. Garnish with basil and serve.

DR NOWZARADAN LUNCH RECIPE
BUTTERNUT SQUASH SOUP WITH AVOCADO & CHICKPEAS
INGREDIENTS

- 1 15-ounce can Amy's Light-in-Sodium Butternut Squash Soup

- ¾ cup canned chickpeas, rinsed

- 1 tablespoon lime juice

- 1 teaspoon curry powder

- Pinch of salt

- 2 tablespoons diced avocado

- 1 tablespoon nonfat plain Greek yogurt

DIRECTIONS

- Step 1

Heat soup in a small saucepan with chickpeas, lime juice, curry powder and salt. To serve, top with avocado and yogurt.

CURRIED CHICKEN APPLE WRAPS
INGREDIENTS

- 1 cup shredded cooked chicken breast

- ½ cup chopped green apple

- 2 tablespoons chopped red onion

- 2 tablespoons light mayonnaise

- 2 tablespoons plain fat-free Greek yogurt

- ¼ teaspoon curry powder

- 2 6- to 7-inch low-carb flour tortillas, such as La Tortilla Factory® brand, warmed (see Tip)

- 12 baby spinach leaves or 2 leaf lettuce leaves

DIRECTIONS

- Step 1

Combine chicken, apple, onion, mayonnaise, yogurt and curry powder in a small bowl.

- Step 2

Line tortillas with spinach (or lettuce). Top with the chicken salad; roll up the tortillas. If desired, secure with toothpicks.

SLOW-COOKER CURRIED BUTTERNUT S□UASH
SOUP
INGREDIENTS

- 1 medium butternut s□uash (2-2 1/2 pounds), peeled, seeded and cubed (about 5 cups)

- 3 cups "no-chicken" broth or vegetable broth

- 1 medium onion, chopped

- 4 teaspoons curry powder

- ½ teaspoon garlic powder

- ¾ teaspoon salt

- 1 (14 ounce) can coconut milk

- 1-2 tablespoons lime juice, plus wedges for serving

- Chopped fresh cilantro for garnish

DIRECTIONS

- Step 1

Stir s☐uash, broth, onion, curry powder, garlic powder and salt together in a 5-quart slow cooker. Cover and cook until the vegetables are very tender, 7 hours on Low or 3 1/2 hours on High. Turn off heat and stir in coconut milk and lime juice to taste. Puree with an immersion blender until smooth. Garnish with cilantro.

SLOW-COOKER VEGETABLE SOUP
INGREDIENTS

- 1 medium onion, chopped

- 2 medium carrots, chopped

43

- 2 stalks celery, chopped

- 12 ounces fresh green beans, cut into 1/2-inch pieces

- 4 cups chopped kale

- 2 medium zucchini, chopped

- 4 Roma tomatoes, seeded and chopped

- 2 cloves garlic, minced

- 2 (15 ounce) cans no-salt-added cannellini or other white beans, rinsed

- 4 cups low-sodium chicken broth or low-sodium vegetable broth

- 1 Parmesan rind (optional)

- 2 teaspoons salt

- ½ teaspoon ground pepper

- 2 teaspoons red-wine vinegar

- 8 teaspoons prepared pesto

DIRECTIONS

- Step 1

Combine onion, carrots, celery, green beans, kale, zucchini, tomatoes, garlic, white beans, broth, Parmesan rind (if using), salt and pepper in a 6-quart or larger slow cooker. Cover and cook on High for 4 hours or Low for 6 hours.

- Step 2

Remove Parmesan rind, if using. Stir in vinegar and top each serving of soup with 1 teaspoon pesto.

KALE SALAD WITH BEETS & WILD RICE

INGREDIENTS

- 1 large bunch lacinato or curly kale, stems trimmed, chopped (8 cups)

- 1 medium beet, peeled, halved and very thinly sliced (2 1/2 cups)

- 1 cup cooked wild rice

- ⅓ cup toasted sunflower seeds

- 5 tablespoons Lemon-Tahini Dressing (see associated recipe)

DIRECTIONS

- Step 1

Combine kale, beet, wild rice and sunflower seeds in a large bowl. Add dressing and toss until well coated. Serve within 2 hours.

WHOLE-WHEAT VEGGIE WRAP

INGREDIENTS

- 1 8-inch whole-wheat tortilla

- 2 tablespoons hummus

- ¼ avocado, mashed

- 1 cup sliced fresh vegetables of your choice

- 2 tablespoons shredded sharp Cheddar cheese

DIRECTIONS

- Step 1

Lay tortilla on work surface. Spread hummus and avocado on the tortilla. Add veggies and Cheddar and roll up. Cut in half before serving

BAGEL AVOCADO TOAST
INGREDIENTS

- ¼ medium avocado, mashed

- 1 slice whole-grain bread, toasted

- 2 teaspoons everything bagel seasoning

- Pinch of flaky sea salt (such as Maldon)

DIRECTIONS

- Step 1

Spread avocado on toast. Top with seasoning and salt.

GREEN SALAD WITH EDAMAME & BEETS
INGREDIENTS

- 2 cups mixed salad greens

- 1 cup shelled edamame, thawed

- ½ medium raw beet, peeled and shredded (about 1/2 cup)

- 1 tablespoon plus 1 1/2 teaspoons red-wine vinegar

- 1 tablespoon chopped fresh cilantro

- 2 teaspoons extra-virgin olive oil

- Freshly ground pepper to taste

DIRECTIONS

- Step 1

Arrange greens, edamame and beet on a large plate. Whisk vinegar, cilantro, oil, salt and pepper in a small bowl. Drizzle over the salad and enjoy.

VEGGIE & HUMMUS SANDWICH

INGREDIENTS

- 2 slices whole-grain bread

- 3 tablespoons hummus

- ¼ avocado, mashed

- ½ cup mixed salad greens

- ¼ medium red bell pepper, sliced

- ¼ cup sliced cucumber

- ¼ cup shredded carrot

DIRECTIONS

- Step 1

Spread one slice of bread with hummus and the other with avocado. Fill the sandwich with greens, bell pepper, cucumber and carrot. Slice in half and serve.

NO-COOK BLACK BEAN SALAD
INGREDIENTS

- ½ cup thinly sliced red onion

- 1 medium ripe avocado, pitted and roughly chopped

- ¼ cup cilantro leaves

- ¼ cup lime juice

- 2 tablespoons extra-virgin olive oil

- 1 clove garlic, minced

- ½ teaspoon salt

- 8 cups mixed salad greens

- 2 medium ears corn, kernels removed, or 2 cups frozen corn, thawed and patted dry

- 1 pint grape tomatoes, halved

- 1 (15 ounce) can black beans, rinsed

DIRECTIONS

- Step 1

Place onion in a medium bowl and cover with cold water. Set aside. Combine avocado, cilantro, lime juice, oil, garlic and salt in a mini food processor. Process, scraping down the sides as needed, until smooth and creamy.

- Step 2

Just before serving, combine salad greens, corn, tomatoes and beans in a large bowl. Drain the onions and add to the bowl, along with the avocado dressing. Toss to coat.

DR NOWZARADAN DINNER RECIPES
CITRUS POACHED SALMON WITH ASPARAGUS
INGREDIENTS

- 4 4-ounce fresh or frozen skinless salmon fillets

- 1 lemon

- 1 orange

- 1 cup water

- 1 pound asparagus spears, woody bases removed

- 2 tablespoons snipped fresh parsley

- 1 tablespoon melted butter

- ¼ teaspoon salt

- ¼ teaspoon ground black pepper

- 1 sprig Fresh parsley leaves

DIRECTIONS

- Step 1

Thaw fish, if frozen. Rinse fish; pat dry with paper towels. Finely shred 1 teaspoon peel from lemon; set aside. Squeeze juice from the lemon and orange; combine juices. Measure 1/4 cup juice for dressing and set aside.

- Step 2

Pour the remaining juice into a large skillet; add water. Bring to boiling. Add salmon; reduce heat to medium. Simmer, covered, for 4 minutes. Lay asparagus atop salmon (see

Tips). Simmer 4 to 8 minutes more or until fish begins to flake when tested with a fork and asparagus is crisp tender.

- Step 3

Meanwhile, in a small bowl combine reserved 1/4 cup juices, snipped parsley, butter, reserved lemon peel, salt and pepper.

- Step 4

To serve, drizzle dressing mixture over salmon and asparagus. Garnish with additional fresh parsley leaves, if desired.

ZUCCHINI NOODLES WITH PESTO & CHICKEN
INGREDIENTS

- 4 medium-large zucchini (about 2 pounds), trimmed

- ¾ teaspoon salt, divided

- 2 cups packed fresh basil leaves

- ¼ cup pine nuts, toasted

- ¼ cup grated Parmesan cheese

- 1/4 cup plus 2 tablespoons extra-virgin olive oil, divided

- 2 tablespoons lemon juice

- 1 large clove garlic, ⬜uartered

- ½ teaspoon ground pepper

- 1 pound boneless, skinless chicken breast, cut into 1-inch pieces

DIRECTIONS

- Step 1

Using a spiral vegetable slicer, cut zucchini lengthwise into long, thin strands. Give the strands a chop here and there so the noodles aren't too long. Place the zucchini in a colander and toss with 1/4 teaspoon salt. Let drain for 15 to 30 minutes, then gently squeeze to remove any excess li☐uid.

- Step 2

Meanwhile, place basil, pine nuts, Parmesan, 1/4 cup oil, lemon juice, garlic, pepper and 1/4 teaspoon salt in a mini food processor. Process until almost smooth.

- Step 3

Heat 1 tablespoon oil in a large skillet over medium-high heat. Add chicken in one layer; sprinkle with the remaining 1/4 teaspoon salt. Cook, stirring, until just cooked through, about 5 minutes. Transfer to a large bowl and stir in 3 tablespoons of the pesto.

- Step 4

Add the remaining 1 tablespoon oil to the pan. Add the drained zucchini noodles and toss gently until hot, 2 to 3 minutes. Transfer to the bowl with the chicken. Add the remaining pesto and toss gently to coat.

SPICY JERK SHRIMP
INGREDIENTS

- 1 ½ pounds fresh or frozen large shrimp in shells

- 4 (1/4 inch thick) slices peeled and cored fresh pineapple, halved

- 2 cups bite-size strips red sweet pepper

- 2 cups sliced red onions

- 1 fresh jalapeño chile pepper, halved lengthwise, seeded and sliced (see Tip)

- 2 tablespoons olive oil

- 1 tablespoon Jamaican jerk seasoning

- ½ cup coarsely snipped fresh cilantro

- 1 ⅓ cups hot cooked brown rice

- Lime wedges

DIRECTIONS

- Step 1

Thaw shrimp, if frozen. Preheat oven to 425 degrees F. Line two 15x10-inch baking pans with foil.

- Step 2

Peel and devein shrimp, leaving tails intact if desired. Rinse shrimp; pat dry. In an extra-large bowl combine shrimp and the next six ingredients (through jerk seasoning); toss gently to coat. Divide mixture between the prepared pans. Roast 15 minutes or until shrimp are opa☐ue.

- Step 3

Sprinkle with cilantro and serve with brown rice and lime wedges.

SHEET-PAN CHICKEN & VEGETABLES WITH ROMESCO SAUCE

INGREDIENTS

- 2 large Yukon Gold potatoes, cubed

- 4 tablespoons extra-virgin olive oil, divided

- 1 teaspoon ground pepper, divided

- ½ teaspoon salt, divided

- 4 bone-in chicken thighs, skin removed, excess fat trimmed

- 4 cups broccoli florets

- 1 (7 ounce) jar roasted red peppers, rinsed

- ¼ cup slivered almonds

- 1 small clove garlic, crushed

- 1 teaspoon paprika

- ½ teaspoon ground cumin

- ¼ teaspoon crushed red pepper

- 2 tablespoons chopped fresh cilantro for garnish

DIRECTIONS

- Step 1

Preheat oven to 450 degrees F.

- Step 2

Toss potatoes with 1 teaspoon oil, 1/4 teaspoon pepper and 1/8 teaspoon salt in a medium bowl. Place on one side of a large rimmed baking sheet. Toss chicken with 1 tablespoon oil, 1/4 teaspoon pepper and 1/8 teaspoon salt in the bowl. Place on the empty side of the baking sheet. Roast for 15 minutes.

• Step 3

Meanwhile, toss broccoli with 2 teaspoons oil, 1/4 teaspoon pepper and 1/8 teaspoon salt in a clean bowl. After the chicken and potatoes have roasted for 10 minutes, add the broccoli to the potato side of the baking sheet. Stir the vegetables together and continue roasting until the chicken is cooked through and the vegetables are tender, about 15 minutes more.

• Step 4

Meanwhile, combine roasted peppers, almonds, garlic, paprika, cumin, crushed red pepper and the remaining 2 tablespoons oil, 1/8 teaspoon salt and 1/4 teaspoon pepper in a mini food processor. Process until fairly smooth.

• Step 5

Serve the chicken and vegetables with the roasted pepper sauce. Sprinkle with cilantro, if desired.

TACO SPAGHETTI S☐UASBOATS
INGREDIENTS

• 2 tablespoons canola oil

• 1 pound ground turkey

• 1 cup chopped onion

- 3 cloves garlic, minced

- 1 medium tomato, chopped

- 4 teaspoons chili powder

- 2 teaspoons ground cumin

- ½ teaspoon salt, divided

- ¼ cup prepared pico de gallo or salsa, plus more for serving

- 1 2 1/2- to 3-pound spaghetti squash, halved lengthwise and seeded

- 1 cup shredded Mexican cheese blend

- 1 cup chopped romaine lettuce

- 1 avocado, chopped

DIRECTIONS

- Step 1

Preheat oven to 450 degrees F.

- Step 2

Heat oil in a large skillet over medium heat. Add turkey, onion and garlic; cook, stirring and breaking the turkey up with a spoon, until no longer pink, 5 to 7 minutes. Add tomato, chili powder, cumin and 1/4 teaspoon salt. Continue cooking and stirring until hot, 2 to 3 minutes more. Remove from heat and stir in pico de gallo (or salsa).

- Step 3

Meanwhile, place squash, cut-side down, in a microwave-safe dish and add 2 tablespoons water. Microwave, uncovered, on High until the flesh is tender, 10 to 15 minutes. (Alternatively, place squash halves, cut-side down, on a rimmed baking sheet. Bake in a 400 degrees F oven until the flesh is tender, 40 to 50 minutes.)

- Step 4

Use a fork to scrape the s☐uash flesh from the shells into the pan with the turkey mixture. Add the remaining 1/4 teaspoon salt and stir to combine. Place the shells on a baking sheet and fill with the squash mixture. Top with cheese. Bake until heated through and the cheese is melted, 10 to 15 minutes. Serve, topped with lettuce, avocado and more pico de gallo (or salsa), if desired.

SHEET-PAN ROASTED SALMON & VEGETABLES
INGREDIENTS

- 1 pound fingerling potatoes, halved lengthwise

- 2 tablespoons olive oil

- 5 garlic cloves, coarsely chopped

- ½ teaspoon sea salt

- ½ teaspoon freshly ground black pepper

- 4 5 to 6-ounce fresh or frozen skinless salmon fillets

- 2 medium red, yellow and/or orange sweet peppers, cut into rings

- 2 cups cherry tomatoes

- 1 ½ cups chopped fresh parsley (1 bunch)

- ¼ cup pitted kalamata olives, halved

- ¼ cup finely snipped fresh oregano or 1 Tbsp. dried oregano, crushed

- 1 lemon

DIRECTIONS

- Step 1

Preheat oven to 425 degrees F. Place potatoes in a large bowl. Drizzle with 1 Tbsp. of the oil and sprinkle with garlic and 1/8 tsp. of the salt and black pepper; toss to coat. Transfer to a 15x10-inch baking pan; cover with foil. Roast 30 minutes.

• Step 2

Meanwhile, thaw salmon, if frozen. Combine, in the same bowl, sweet peppers, tomatoes, parsley, olives, oregano and 1/8 tsp. of the salt and black pepper. Drizzle with remaining 1 Tbsp. oil; toss to coat.

• Step 3

Rinse salmon; pat dry. Sprinkle with remaining 1/4 tsp. salt and black pepper. Spoon sweet pepper mixture over potatoes and top with salmon. Roast, uncovered, 10 minutes more or just until salmon flakes.

- Step 4

Remove zest from lemon. Squeeze juice from lemon over salmon and vegetables. Sprinkle with zest.

EASY BROWN RICE
INGREDIENTS

- 2 ½ cups water or broth

- 1 cup brown rice

DIRECTIONS

- Step 1

Combine water (or broth) and rice in a medium saucepan. Bring to a boil. Reduce heat to low, cover and simmer until tender and most of the liquidhas been absorbed, 40 to 50 minutes. Let stand 5 minutes, then fluff with a fork.

CRISPY OVEN-FRIED FISH TACOS
INGREDIENTS

- Cooking spray

- 1 cup whole-grain cereal flakes

- ¾ cup dry whole-wheat breadcrumbs

- ¾ teaspoon ground pepper, divided

- ½ teaspoon garlic powder

- ½ teaspoon paprika

- ½ teaspoon salt, divided

- ½ cup all-purpose flour

- 2 large egg whites

- 2 tablespoons water

- 1 pound cod, cut into 1/2-by-3-inch strips (cut in half horizontally, if very thick)

- 2 tablespoons avocado oil

- 2 tablespoons unseasoned rice vinegar

- 3 cups coleslaw mix

- 1 avocado, diced

- 8 corn tortillas, warmed

- Pico de gallo

DIRECTIONS

- Step 1

Preheat oven to 450 degrees F. Set a wire rack on a baking sheet; coat with cooking spray.

- Step 2

71

Place cereal flakes, breadcrumbs, 1/2 teaspoon pepper, garlic powder, paprika and 1/4 teaspoon salt in a food processor and process until finely ground. Transfer to a shallow dish.

- Step 3

Place flour in a second shallow dish. Whisk egg whites and water together in a third shallow dish. Dredge each piece of fish in the flour, dip it in the egg white mixture and then coat on all sides with the breadcrumb mixture. Place on the prepared rack. Coat both sides of the breaded fish with cooking spray. Bake until the fish is cooked through and the breading is golden brown and crisp, about 10 minutes.

- Step 4

Meanwhile, whisk oil, vinegar and the remaining 1/4 teaspoon each pepper and salt in a medium bowl. Add coleslaw mix and toss to coat.

- Step 5

Divide the fish, coleslaw mix and avocado evenly among tortillas. Serve with pico de gallo, if desired.

GARLIC-LIME PORK WITH FARRO & SPINACH
INGREDIENTS

- 3 tablespoons lime juice

- 1 tablespoon peanut butter or almond butter

- 4 cloves garlic, minced

- 1 ½ teaspoons honey

- ½ teaspoon salt

- ½ teaspoon black pepper

- 4 (8 ounce) bone-in pork chops, cut 3/4 to 1 inch thick and trimmed

- 4 teaspoons olive oil

- 1 8.5-ounce pouch cooked farro, such as Simply Balanced™

- 2 (5 ounce) packages fresh baby spinach

- 2 tablespoons chopped walnuts, toasted (see Tip) (Optional)

- 1 wedge Lime wedges

DIRECTIONS

- Step 1

In a small bowl whisk together lime juice, peanut butter, garlic, honey, 1/4 teaspoon of the salt and 1/4 teaspoon of the pepper. Sprinkle chops with the remaining 1/4 teaspoon salt and pepper.

• Step 2

In a 12-inch nonstick skillet heat 2 teaspoon of the oil over medium-high. Add chops; cook 7 to 10 minutes or until a thermometer registers 145 degrees F, turning once. Remove from skillet; cover and keep warm.

• Step 3

In same skillet heat the remaining 2 teaspoon oil over medium. Add lime mixture, stirring to scrape up crusty brown bits. Add farro; cook and stir until grains are separated. Add spinach; cook and stir until heated through and spinach is beginning to wilt. If desired, season with additional pepper.

- Step 4

Serve chops with farro mixture. If desired, sprinkle with walnuts and serve with lime wedges.

VEGAN COCONUT CHICKPEA CURRY
INGREDIENTS

- 2 teaspoons avocado oil or canola oil

- 1 cup chopped onion

- 1 cup diced bell pepper

- 1 medium zucchini, halved and sliced

- 1 (15 ounce) can chickpeas, drained and rinsed

- 1 ½ cups coconut curry simmer sauce (see Tip)

- ½ cup vegetable broth

- 4 cups baby spinach

- 2 cups precooked brown rice, heated according to package instructions

DIRECTIONS

- Step 1

Heat oil in a large skillet over medium-high heat. Add onion, pepper and zucchini; cook, stirring often, until the vegetables begin to brown, 5 to 6 minutes.

- Step 2

Add chickpeas, simmer sauce and broth and bring to a simmer, stirring. Reduce heat to medium-low and simmer until the vegetables are tender, 4 to 6 minutes. Stir in spinach just before serving. Serve over rice.

CONCLUSION

The Dr. Nowzaradan Diet, or Dr. Now Diet, is a restrictive, 1,200 calorie diet designed to promote rapid weight loss in people who are about to undergo weight loss surgery.

While it does have its place in certain medical contexts, it's not for most people — and certainly not a suitable option if you're looking for a diet that you can stick with long term to promote slow and sustainable weight loss.

The diet should also be done under medical supervision.

Made in United States
Troutdale, OR
03/02/2024

18107205R00046